Explore Ancient Greece

Zelda Wagner

Lerner Publications ◆ Minneapolis

Lerner Publications Company
An imprint of Lerner Publishing Group, Inc.
241 First Avenue North
Minneapolis, MN 55401 USA

For reading levels and more information, look up this title at www.lernerbooks.com.

Main body text set in Billy Infant Regular. Typeface provided by SparkyType.

Editor: Angel Kidd
Lerner team: Sue Marquis

Library of Congress Cataloging-in-Publication Data

Names: Wagner, Zelda, 2000- author
Title: Explore ancient Greece / Zelda Wagner.
Description: Minneapolis, MN : Lerner Publications, [2026] | Series: Lightning bolt books - early civilizations | Includes bibliographical references and index. | Audience: Ages 6-9 | Audience: Grades 2-3 | Summary: "The ancient Greeks were great warriors, artists, and learners. Curious readers will discover the polytheistic religion, many forms of art, democratic government, and common warfare of ancient Greece"— Provided by publisher.
Identifiers: LCCN 2025015756 (print) | LCCN 2025015757 (ebook) | ISBN 9798765689271 library binding | ISBN 9798348028961 paperback | ISBN 9798765696781 epub
Subjects: LCSH: Greece—Civilization—To 146 B.C.—Juvenile literature | Greece—Historical geography—Juvenile literature
Classification: LCC DF77 .W34 2026 (print) | LCC DF77 (ebook) | DDC 938—dc23/eng/20250709

LC record available at https://lccn.loc.gov/2025015756
LC ebook record available at https://lccn.loc.gov/2025015757

Manufactured in the United States of America
1-1012504-54795-8/7/2025

Table of Contents

Land and Sea

The ancient Greek civilization began more than four thousand years ago. A civilization is a group of people who live in the same area and share a culture.

Ancient Greece was in Southeastern Europe and covered with mountains. Traveling on foot or horseback was hard.

Some Greek battles were fought at sea.

Water surrounded ancient Greece on three sides. The Greeks were skilled sailors and traveled by sea.

Greece was home to the world's first democracy. In a democracy, people get to vote on their leaders and many of their laws.

People voted in buildings like this one.

Greece had many city-states. Two of the largest were Athens and Sparta. About 2,500 years ago, many Greek city-states joined together to fight Persia during a war.

This temple was built near Athens.

Daily Life

Many ancient Greeks were farmers who grew crops and raised animals. Some Greeks were fishers, builders, artists, athletes, or teachers. Men and women had different jobs.

Men talked about art and science and voted on laws. They threw parties and went to the theater. They also spent time training as soldiers.

All Spartan men were soldiers.

Sewing was an important task for Greek women.

Most Greek women did housework and raised children. Some women were not allowed to go outside often. **But women in Sparta had more freedom.**

Art was important to the Greeks. There were many great painters, potters, sculptors, actors, and musicians.

The Greeks believed gods controlled Earth. The people built temples to honor their gods. They had many myths about their gods and heroes.

The Parthenon was built to honor the goddess Athena.

The Greek alphabet has twenty-four letters. Ancient Greeks wrote on wax-covered tablets made of wood or ivory. They used a writing tool called a stylus to form the letters.

α	Alpha
β	Beta
γ	Gamma
δ	Delta
ϵ	Epsīlon
ζ	Zeta
η	Eta
θ	Theta
ι	Iōta
κ	Kappa
λ	Lambda
μ	Mu
ν	Nu
ξ	Xi
ο	Omīcron
π	Pi
ρ	Rho
σ	Sigma
τ	Tau
υ	Upsīlon
ϕ	Phi
χ	Chi (Ki)
ψ	Psi
ω	Omĕga

The Greek alphabet

A tablet from ancient Greece

Boys learned to write in school. Adults wrote stories about heroes and gods. They also sent letters to one another.

Fall of Greece

About eighteen years after the war against Persia, Athens and Sparta fought each other. The war lasted twenty-seven years. Sparta won, but the fighting weakened all of Greece.

Alexander the Great ruled Greece sixty-eight years after the war. His armies took over many lands. Greece became one of the largest empires in ancient history.

Alexander the Great

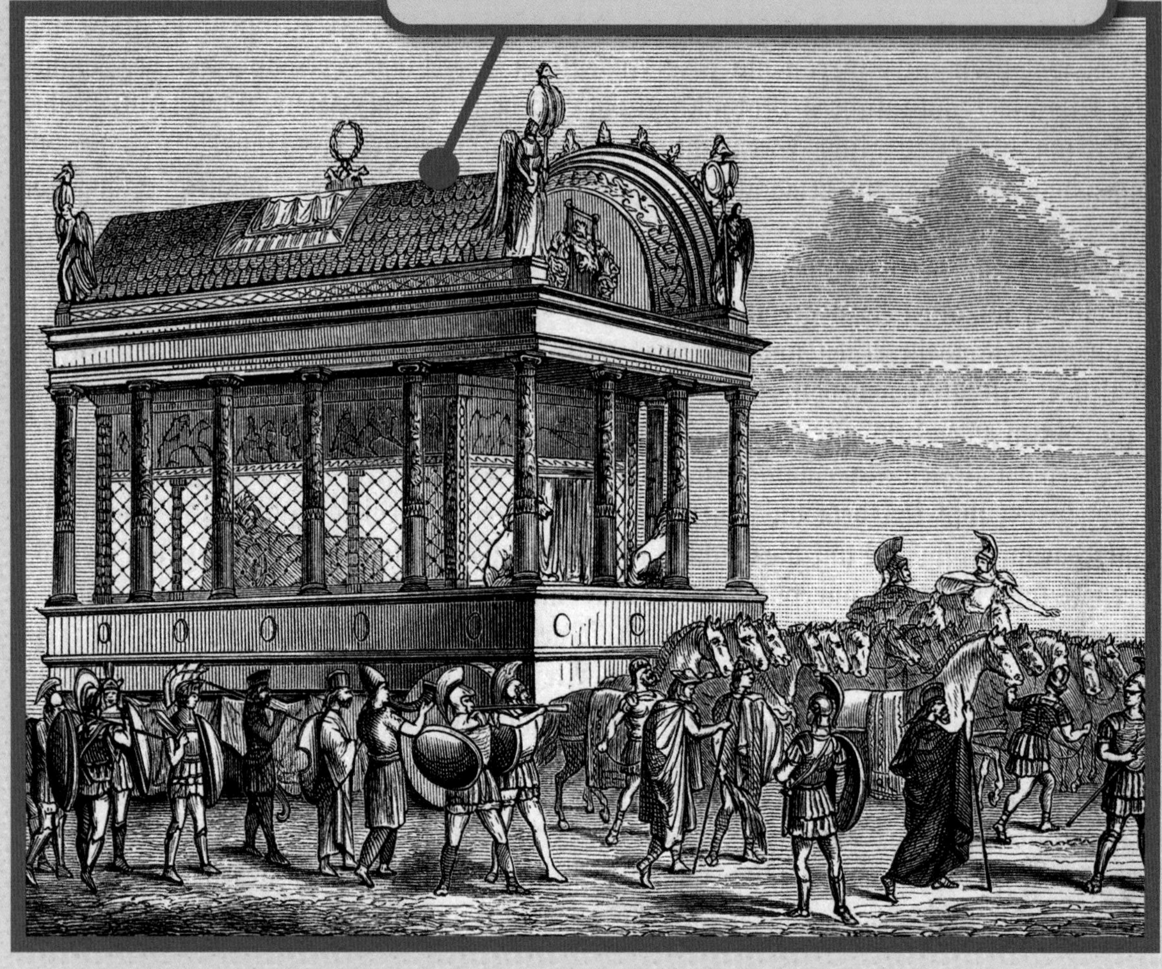

When Alexander died, many people wanted to take over as the ruler. They fought one another, and the empire was torn apart.

About one hundred and eighty years later, Rome took over Greece. The Romans borrowed many things from the Greeks, including art, religion, and democracy.

Greek men bow to a Roman general

A Look at the Olympic Games

The ancient Greeks played many sports. Young men wrestled, boxed, ran races, and competed in the long jump. They threw javelins and discuses.

The Greeks held the first Olympic Games about 2,800 years ago. These games were very different from the modern Olympics. Only men could compete. The winners' prizes were wreaths made from olive leaves.

Ancient Greece Facts

- Zeus is the king of the Greek gods. He is the god of the sky.
- The Greek myth of Icarus is about a boy who made wax wings and flew too close to the sun.
- Aristotle was a famous Greek thinker. He tutored Alexander the Great for about eight years.

Glossary

ancient: very old

city-state: a self-governing city and the lands it controls

civilization: a large group of people who live in an area and share a common government and culture

culture: the beliefs, practices, and acts of everyday life shared by people in a particular place or time

democracy: a type of government where citizens vote for leaders and laws

empire: a group of nations or peoples under one ruler or government

ivory: a material that comes from elephant and walrus tusks

myth: a story often told to teach a lesson or to explain history, beliefs, or something else

potter: a person who makes pottery

Learn More

Britannica Kids: Alexander the Great
https://kids.britannica.com/kids/article/Alexander-the-Great/352726

Ha, Christine. *Zeus*. Apex, 2022.

Havemeyer, Janie. *A Day in Ancient Greece*. Grasshopper, 2025.

Kiddle: Ancient Greece Facts for Kids
https://kids.kiddle.co/Ancient_Greece

Kiddle: Parthenon Facts for Kids
https://kids.kiddle.co/Parthenon

Wagner, Zelda. *Explore Ancient Rome*. Lerner Publications, 2026.

Index

Photo Acknowledgments

Image credits: Salvator Barki/Getty Images, p. 4; Laura Westlund/Independent Picture Service, p. 5; mikroman6/Getty Images, p. 6; Iñigo Fdz de Pinedo/Getty Images, p. 7; Guven Ozdemir/Getty Images, p. 8; Werner Forman/Getty Images, p. 9; Universal History Archive/Getty Images, pp. 10, 20; North Wind Picture Archives/Alamy, p. 11; arsenisspyros/Getty Images, p. 12; joe daniel price/Getty Images, p. 13; mikroman6/Getty Images, p. 14; Craig Pershouse/Getty Images, p. 15; INTERFOTO/Alamy, p. 16; Hulton Archive/Getty Images, p. 17; Stock Montage/Getty Images, p. 18; Bob Thomas/Popperfoto/Getty Images, p. 19.

Cover: Richmatts/Getty Images.